Nice to Meet You... Let's Be Friends

By Dr. Peggy Ferguson

Nice to Meet You...
Let's Be Friends

Copyright © 2020 by Peggy Ferguson

ISBN (978-1-63649-644-3)

Dedication

To my grandchildren, and all the children of the world...
always be kind and excited about meeting new friends.

Excitedly, Mason and his younger brother Caden were discussing friends.

I sat down with them and we had a lively conversation about friends.

One day while playing outside on
the playground, one of Mason's friends
pushed him. Caden said, "That's not
nice to push your friend."
Mason agreed and replied, "No, it's not kind
to push someone, especially your friend."

Mason thought, "I will sit down with my friends and tell them about the talk we had about friends."

Caden responded, "Good idea, Mason!"
and they gave each other high fives.

How do we make new friends?

We meet new people everyday.

We exchange introductions.

We ask each other
"get-to-know-you" questions.

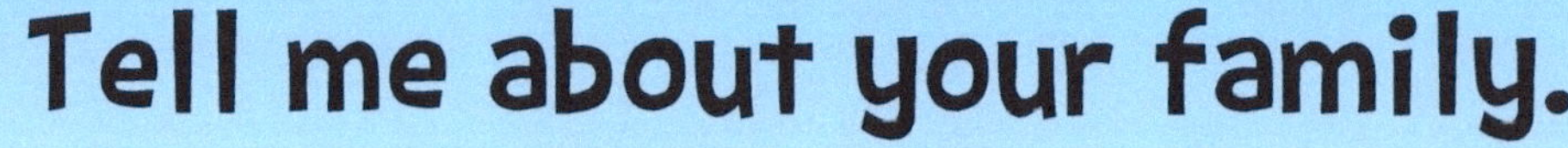

Tell me about your family.

I welcome my new friend with a hug.

We share laughs together.

My friend helps me
when I need assistance.

My friend shares with me.

When we see each other again,
we greet one another.

My new friend asks how I'm feeling.

My new friend encourages me.

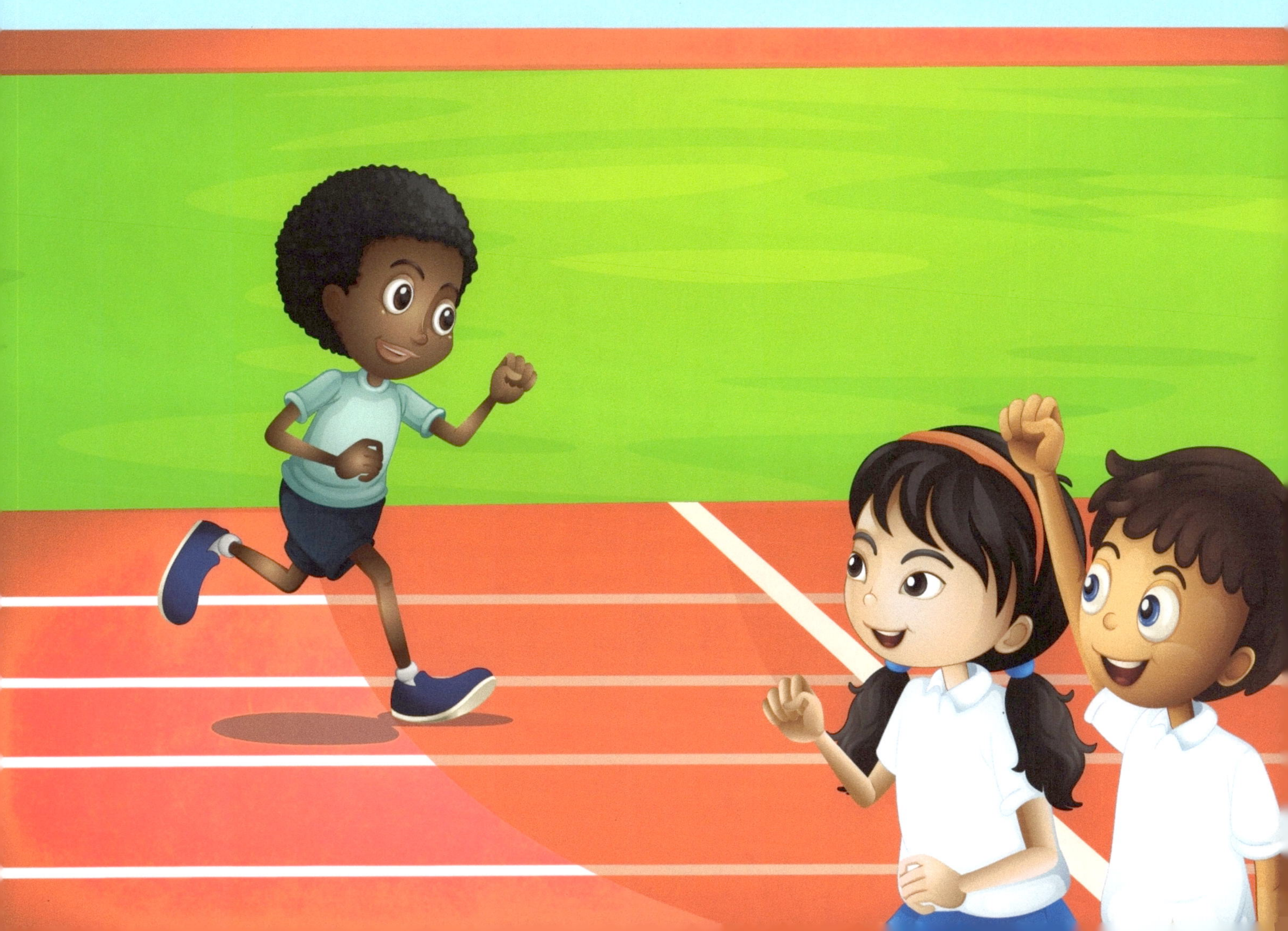

My new friend compliments me.

My new friend dances with me.

My new friend sings with me.

My new friend trusts me.

My new friend believes I am special.

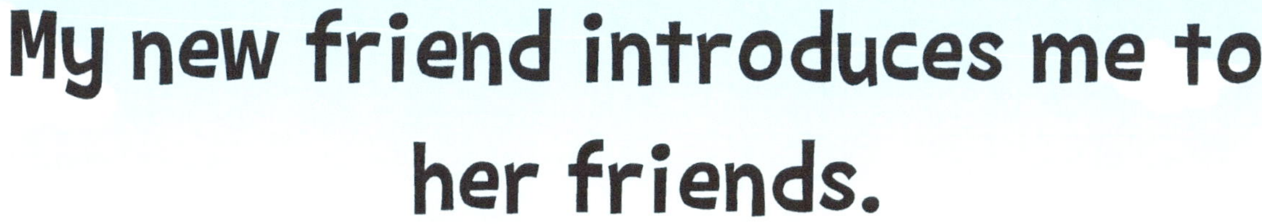

My new friend introduces me to her friends.

My friends are boys and girls.

I greet them with a smile.

Our conversation shows our similarities.

Now we know a little more
about each other.

My new friends help me see
things from a different perspective.

We say our goodbyes when
we depart.

Have you made any new
friends lately?

My New Friend Shows Their Gratitude for
Our Friendship Through…

Love
Joy
Peace
Patience
Kindness
Goodness
Gentleness
Loyalty
Self-control

Friendship Affirmations

I will encourage others.

I will be patient with others.

I will be kind.

I will be honest.

I will be positive.

I will say 'no' if I have to.

I will be a good listener.

I will be a good helper.

I will be respectful.